WRITING
Words that Wow!

Wonderful Words You Should Use

Student Resource and Writing Workbook

Grades 3-5

By Darlene Dehart Bingham

Welcome to Writing Words that *Wow!*

Writing Words that Wow! is a student resource and writing workbook that teaches young writers how to make wise word choices. The workbook contains numerous lesson plans, word lists, and examples that show students how to avoid dull, overused words, and instead, chose wonderful words that create sizzling, sensational sentences.

Tutortime4kidz Resources

tutortime4kidz@yahoo.com

ISBN-10: 0-9986382-1-8

ISBN-13: 978-0-9986382-1-8

All rights reserved.

Printed in the U.S.A.

Table of Contents

Use Exact Nouns

Nouns are words that name people, animals, places, things, and ideas. Avoid using general nouns by using exact common nouns and proper nouns in sentences.

	General Noun	Examples of Exact Nouns
People:	athlete	soccer player, tennis player, wrestler
Animals:	dog	Akita, Dalmatian, German shepherd
Place:	park	New York Central Park, Washington Park
Thing:	flower	daffodil, daisy, rose, tulip

Examples of Replacing General Nouns with Exact Common Nouns:

The **car** screeched to a sudden stop.
Car is a general noun.
The **ambulance** screeched to a sudden stop.
Ambulance is a better choice because it describes what kind of car or vehicle.

Dad bought Mom a dozen red **flowers** for Mother's Day.
Flowers is a general noun.
Dad bought Mom a dozen red **roses** for Mother's Day.
Roses is an exact noun.

Julian loves to play **sports**. *Sports is a general noun.*
Julian loves to play **football** and **soccer**. *Football and soccer are exact nouns.*

Examples of Replacing General Nouns with Exact Proper Nouns:

The **man** gave a speech at the university. *Man is a general noun.*
Mayor Andrew Patton gave a speech at the university.
Mayor Andrew Patton is an exact proper noun.

The **dog** chased the squirrel up the oak tree. *Dog is a general noun.*
The **Dalmatian** chased the squirrel up the oak tree. *Dalmatian is an exact proper noun.*

Shirley climbed the face of the **mountain**. *Mountain is a general noun.*
Shirley climbed the face of **Mount Everest**. *Mount Everest is an exact proper noun.*

Use Exact Nouns
Avoid General Nouns and Use Exact Nouns

GENERAL	EXACT NOUN WORD LIST
People	**Words to Use**
athlete	baseball player, boxer, football player, rugby player, soccer player, softball player, swimmer, tennis player, wrestler
boy	baby boy, boyfriend, brother, infant boy, nephew, prince, teenage boy, ten-year-old boy, twin brother, younger brother
girl	baby girl, daughter, girlfriend, older sister, one-year-old girl, princess, sister, teenage girl, twin sister, younger sister
man	brother, dad, father, gentleman, grand-father, grandpa, husband, king, papa, patriarch, uncle
people	actor, dentist, doctor, fire fighter, football fan, nurse, parent, patient, pilot, police officer, principal, student, teacher
specific people	Aunt Minerva, Dad, Governor Brown, Mayor Connolly, Mom, President Lincoln, Principal Hines, Reverend Mays, Uncle Henry
woman	aunt, grandma, grand-mother, lady, mama, matriarch, mom, mother, queen, sister, wife
Animals	**Words to Use**
bear	black bear, brown bear, grizzly bear, panda, polar bear
bird	dove, hummingbird, peacock, penguin, robin, swallow
butterfly	monarch, Painted Lady, Red Admiral, swallowtail
cat	American shorthair, calico, Manx, Persian, Siamese, tabby
dog	Akita, American bulldog, beagle, Border collie, Dalmatian, German shepherd, Labrador retriever, Irish setter, poodle
farm animals	chickens, cows, goats, hens, lamb, pigs, rooster
fish	barracuda, goldfish, marlin, salmon, sailfish, tuna
horse	Appaloosa, Arabian, Clydesdale, mustang, Shetland pony
insect	ant, bee, beetle, cricket, fly, grasshopper, ladybug, mosquito
jungle animal	cheetah, elephant, giraffe, lion, monkey, tiger, zebra
snake	cobra, copperhead, coral, mamba, python, rattlesnake

Use Exact Nouns
Avoid General Nouns and Use Exact Nouns

GENERAL	EXACT NOUN WORD LIST
Places	**Words to Use**
amusement park	Disneyland, Disney World, Legoland, Sea World, Six Flags Magic Kingdom, Universal Studios
building	bakery, bank, church, factory, farm house, gas station, haunted house, high school gym, hotel, library, office, stadium, temple
specific building or structure	Buckingham Palace, Eiffel Tower, Empire State Building, Great Wall of China, Hilton Hotel, Statue of Liberty, Taj Mahal, The White House
city	Beijing, Boston, Chicago, Honolulu, London, New York, Paris, San Francisco, Seoul, Tokyo
country	Argentina, Brazil, Canada, China, Egypt, France, Germany, India, Italy, Japan, Mexico, Russia, Spain, United Kingdom, United States
lake	Lake Amador, Lake Michigan, Lake Ontario, Lake Powell, Lake Superior, Lake Tahoe
library	Boston Public Library, Dougherty Valley Library, New York City Library
mountain	Mt. Everest, Mt. Whitney, Rocky Mountains, Sierra Nevada, Swiss Alps
national park	Grand Canyon National Park, Sequoia National Park, Yellowstone National Park, Yosemite National Park
ocean	Arctic Ocean, Atlantic Ocean, Indian Ocean, Pacific Ocean
school	Portland High School, Springtown Elementary School, Valley High School
store	book store, department store, grocery store, hardware store, shoe store, sporting goods store, supermarket, toy store
vacation spot	Aspen, Grand Canyon, Hilton Head, Lake Tahoe, Las Vegas, Maui, Orlando Beach, Palm Springs, Santa Cruz, Time Square, Waikiki Beach

Use Exact Nouns
Avoid General Nouns and Use Exact Nouns

GENERAL	EXACT NOUN WORD LIST
Things	**Words to Use**
book	Black Beauty, Charlotte's Web, Island of the Blue Dolphin
breakfast food	bacon, bagel, cereal, eggs, oatmeal, pancake, toast, waffle
car	ambulance, BMW, cab, convertible, Lexus sedan, limousine, Mercedes SUV, mini-van, police car, race car, sports car, station wagon, SUV, taxicab, van
dessert	apple pie, carrot cake, chocolate brownie, cupcakes, hot fudge sundae, ice cream, lemon bars, pumpkin pie, sugar cookies, vanilla pudding
dinner food	cheese pizza, chicken, hamburger, lasagna, steak, taco, tamales
drink	apple juice, coke, cranberry juice, lemonade, milk, orange juice, 7-up, root beer, water, wine
flower	carnation, daisy, daffodil, iris, lily, rose, sunflower, tulip
fruit	apple, banana, grapes, orange, peach, pear, watermelon
instrument	drums, guitar, keyboard, piano, trombone, trumpet, violin
lunch food	cheese pizza, hamburger, peanut butter sandwich, salad, tomato soup, taco, tuna sandwich
money	coins, dime, dollar, five dollars, nickel, penny, quarter
music	country, gospel, jazz, pop, rap, rock, rock & blues, soul
nut	almond, coconut, hazelnut, peanut, pecan, walnut
planet	Earth, Jupiter, Mars, Mercury, Neptune, Saturn, Uranus, Venus
snack	corn chips, crackers, peanuts, popcorn, potato chips, pretzels, sunflower seeds
sport	baseball, basketball, boxing, football, rugby, soccer, softball
tool	drill, hammer, pliers, saw, screw driver, wire cutters, wrench
toy	fidget spinner, Frisbee, Hot Wheels, hula hoop, Legos, Lincoln Logs, Pokémon, Tinkertoy, Tonka truck, yo-yo
tree	apple, birch, lemon, maple, pine, oak, redwood, willow
vegetable	asparagus, broccoli, carrots, corn, green beans, lettuce
vehicle (not car)	airplane, bus, cruise ship, motorcycle, sail boat, train, truck

Use Exact Nouns

Now You Try!

Add an exact noun to each sentence below. Use the *Exact Noun Word List* on pages 3-5 if you need help.

Example: Veronica walked the _poodle_ puppy for one mile. **(Dog)**

1. I love to eat _____ for dinner. **(Food)**

2. Tia watched the _____ land on the grass. **(Insect)**

3. The _____ wore a diamond crown to the ball. **(Girl)**

4. The _____ roared loudly. **(Animal)**

5. Fran sped down the highway in her _____. **(Car)**

6. Manny gave Danielle a beautiful _____. **(Flower)**

7. Ben used a _____ to build a new dog house. **(Tool)**

8. Sarina bought a _____ at the local pet store. **(Cat)**

9. Chad enjoys playing _____. **(Sport)**

10. The hospital was filled with many _____. **(People)**

Write It

Write 2 sentences using exact nouns.

1. _____

_____

2. _____

_____

Use Amazing Adjectives

Adjectives are words that describe nouns and pronouns. They tell what kind, what color, how many, or which one. Avoid using dull adjectives by using amazing adjectives to describe nouns and pronouns.

Examples:	Dull Adjectives	Example of Amazing Adjectives
What Kind:	*big* elephant	*huge African* elephant
What Color:	*red* wagon	*cherry red* wagon
How Many:	*a lot* of flies	*hundreds* of flies
Which One:	*those* frogs	*ten green* frogs

Adjectives are usually placed before or after the noun or pronoun they describe.

Example:

The **huge African** elephant chased the **wild** monkey up an **oak** tree.

Common Adjectives Begin with a Lower Case Letter

Examples of Using Common Adjectives:

The whale skimmed above the surface of the Pacific Ocean. *No adjectives.*

The **enormous gray** whale skimmed above the surface of the Pacific Ocean.

The adjectives describe the size and color of the whale.

Proper Adjectives Begin with an Upper Case Letter

Proper adjectives are formed from proper nouns often related to a country or cultural name. They begin with an upper case letter.

Examples of Proper Adjectives:

African safari, **American** cheese, **Chinese** food, **French** fries, **German** chocolate, **Italian** bread, **Mexican** food, **Swiss** cheese

Examples of Using Proper Adjectives:

Mom baked a **German** chocolate cake for dessert.

Bruce ordered **French** fries at the restaurant.

Adele bought **Swiss** cheese at the grocery store.

Use Amazing Adjectives
Avoid Dull Words and Use Amazing Adjectives

DULL	AMAZING ADJECTIVE WORD LIST
Colors	**Words to Use**
black	charcoal, coal, ebony, graphite, jet-black, licorice, midnight black, onyx, pitch-black, slate
blue	aqua, baby blue, blue-green, denim, indigo, light blue, navy blue, peacock blue, royal blue, sapphire, sky blue, teal, turquoise
brown	beige, bronze, brunette, caramel, chestnut, coffee, copper, khaki, mocha, nutmeg, oak, tan, teak, toast, walnut
gray/grey	ash, cloud gray, concrete gray, lead, oyster, shadowy gray, silvery, slate gray, smoky gray, steel, stone
green	apple, avocado, chartreuse, emerald, evergreen, fern, forest green, jade, lime, mint, mossy, sage, seaweed
orange	amber, apricot, bronze, carrot, copper, coral, ginger, light orange, peach, pumpkin, tangerine, terra cotta
pink	coral, dark pink, fuchsia, hot pink, light pink, magenta, mauve
purple	fuchsia, grape, lavender, light purple, lilac, mauve, orchid, periwinkle, plum, violet, violet red, wine
red	berry, blood-red, brick red, candy apple, cherry red, crimson, fiery, magenta, maroon, rose, ruby, scarlet, strawberry, wine
white	alabaster, blond, chalky, chiffon, cream, ghost white, ivory, marshmallow, pearl, snow-white
yellow	amber, banana, butter, butterscotch, canary, gold, golden, honey, lemon, light yellow, mustard, sunset, topaz
multicolor	brindle, calico, colorful, kaleidoscope, rainbow, speckled, tabby
Shades	**Words to Use**
bright	ablaze, aglow, blazing, brilliant, dazzling, fiery, flashing, flickering, glazed, gleaming, glimmering, glistening, glittering, glittery, glowing, golden, jeweled, illuminated, luminous, lustrous, moonlit, polished, radiant, shiny, sparkling, sparkly, starry, sunny, twinkling, vivid
clear	cloudless, crystal, crystal clear, glassy, glossy, see-through, sheer, translucent, transparent
dull	bleak, bleary, blurry, cloudy, dim, dingy, dismal, drab, dreary, dusky, faded, foggy, gloomy, gray, hazy, lackluster, moonless, muddy, murky, shadowy, sooty, sunless

Use Amazing Adjectives
Avoid Dull Words and Use Amazing Adjectives

DULL	AMAZING ADJECTIVE WORD LIST
Sizes	Words to Use
big	colossal, enormous, giant, gigantic, huge, humongous, husky, immense, jumbo, massive, mammoth, monstrous, towering, vast
heavy	ample, beefy, bulky, chubby, chunky, hefty, huge, massive, obese, overweight, plump, stocky, stout, weighty
short	compact, diminutive, dwarfed, little, petite, pint-size, puny, slight, stunted, tiny, undersized
small	bite-size, dainty, miniature, munchkin, petite, pint-size, puny, teensy, teeny, tiny
tall	beanstalk, gigantic, lanky, overgrown, sky-high, statuesque, towering
thin	beanpole, bony, feeble, frail, gaunt, lanky, lean, scrawny, skeletal, skinny, slender, slight, stick, trim, twig
Shapes	Words to Use
curved shapes	ball-shaped, bubble, circular, crescent, cylindrical, disk-shaped, dome-shaped, egg-shaped, elliptical, oval, ring, round, sphere
other	box-shaped, cone-shaped, cube, diamond-shaped, four-sided, heart-shaped, rectangular, square, star-shaped, triangular
More Words	Words to Use
afraid	alarmed, distressed, fearful, frightened, horrified, panicky, petrified, quivery, scared, shaky, skittish, terrified, timid, uneasy, weakened, worried
bad	awful, cruel, dreadful, evil, grim, gruesome, hideous, horrible, naughty, obnoxious, vicious, wicked
brave	adventurous, bold, chivalrous, confident, courageous, daring, fearless, gallant, heroic, undaunted, valiant
clean	bright, flawless, fresh, immaculate, laundered, neat, sparkling, spick-and-span, spotless, uncluttered, unsoiled, untainted, washed, white
cold	arctic, bitter, brisk, chilly, cool, crisp, freezing, frigid, frosty, frozen, ice-cold, icy, numbing, polar, refreshing, refrigerated, snowy, wintry

Use Amazing Adjectives
Avoid Dull Words and Use Amazing Adjectives

DULL	AMAZING ADJECTIVE WORD LIST
More Words	Words to Use
dirty	dusty, filthy, greasy, grimy, grubby, messy, muddy, polluted, scummy, slimy, smudged, soiled, sooty, straggly, untidy, unwashed
fast	accelerated, dashing, flashing, fluttering, flying, hurried, quick, racing, rapid, speedy, streaked, swift
fun	enjoying, entertaining, exciting, humorous, playful, silly, witty
good	amazing, awesome, excellent, exceptional, fabulous, fantastic, great, magnificent, marvelous, sensational, spectacular, super, superb
happy	cheerful, delighted, delightful, elated, excited, gleeful, jolly, joyful, jubilant, overjoyed, perky, sunny, thrilled, tickled
hard	crisp, dense, firm, inflexible, iron, rigid, rocklike, solid, stiff, stony
hot	baking, blazing, blistering, boiling, broiling, burning, flaming, muggy, piping hot, roasting, scorching, sizzling, steaming, sweltering, tepid, toasty, torrid, tropical
light (weight)	airy, buoyant, featherweight, feathery, lightweight, weightless
mad	agitated, angry, crazy, cross, enraged, fiery, frantic, furious, heated, infuriated, meltdown, outraged, unglued
new	brand-new, cutting edge, fashionable, fresh, modern, state-of-the-art, recent, trendy, unused, up-to-date, young, youthful
nice	agreeable, amiable, charming, easygoing, friendly, generous, good-hearted, good-natured, helpful, kind, likeable, pleasant, polite
old	aged, ancient, antique, broken-down, dated, elderly, historic, old-fashioned, prehistoric, ragged, run-down, worn, wrinkled, wrinkly
poor	bankrupt, dirt poor, impoverished, moneyless, needy, penniless
pretty	adorable, attractive, beautiful, dazzling, glamorous, good-looking, gorgeous, handsome, radiant, ravishing, striking, stunning

Use Amazing Adjectives
Avoid Dull Words and Use Amazing Adjectives

DULL	AMAZING ADJECTIVE WORD LIST
More Words	Words to Use
rough	bumpy, choppy, coarse, craggy, crumbling, grainy, gravelly, gritty, jagged, knotty, lumpy, prickly, ragged, rocky, sandy, scratchy, uneven
sad	bitter, brokenhearted, crushed, dejected, depressed, devastated, gloomy, grief-stricken, heartbroken, melancholy, somber, troubled
sharp	jagged, knifelike, pointy, prickly, razor-sharp, sharp-edged, spiky, thorny
slow	crawling, gradual, inching, lazy, snail's pace, unhurried
smart	bright, brilliant, clever, ingenious, intelligent, knowledgeable, wise
soft	brittle, creamy, cushioned, delicate, doughy, feathery, flimsy, fluffy, furry, mushy, puffy, silky, snuggly, spongy, squishy, velvety
sour (taste)	bitter, lemony, limey, tangy, tart
spiced	barbecued, cinnamon, curried, fiery, garlicky, hot, peppery, seasoned, spicy, salty, sautéed, well-seasoned, zesty
strange	bizarre, crazy, creepy, curious, frightful, horrid, odd, weird
strong	athletic, brawny, energetic, forceful, mighty, muscular, powerful, sturdy, tough, well-built
sweet (taste)	candied, chocolaty, flavorful, fruity, honeyed, rich, sugar coated, sugary, sweetened, syrupy
talented	artistic, brilliant, creative, experienced, gifted, ingenious, skilled
tired	beat, drained, exhausted, faint, fatigued, sleepy, weary
wet	clammy, damp, dewy, drizzling, humid, misty, moist, rainy, slimy, slippery, slushy, soaked, soggy, sticky, stormy, waterlogged
wonderful	amazing, awesome, extraordinary, fabulous, fascinating, glorious, incredible, magnificent, marvelous, sensational, spectacular, super, superb, terrific, unbelievable

Use Amazing Adjectives

Now You Try!
Place an amazing adjective in each sentence below. Use the *Amazing Adjective Word List* on pages 8-11 if you need help.
Example: Kenzley sipped the <u>chocolate</u> milkshake.

1. The ocean waves crashed onto the _____ beach.

2. Tia felt _____ when she won the spelling bee.

3. The queen wore a _____ crown on her head.

4. Marisa held the _____ kitten in her lap.

5. Edison licked the _____ candy cane.

6. Jennifer baked _____ chocolate chip cookies.

7. Rosa watched the _____ sun rise over the hills.

8. The princess wore a _____ gown to the ball.

9. The _____ kangaroo hopped toward the tourist.

10. Evan carefully climbed up the _____ cliff.

Write It
Write 2 sentences using amazing adjectives to describe exact nouns.

1. _____

_____

2. _____

_____

Use Commas Between Equal Adjectives

Use commas between equal adjectives. If the adjectives are side-by-side and they "equally" describe the same noun, then a comma is needed between the adjectives. To determine if the adjectives are "equal," try reversing them. If the sentence flows well and makes sense, then the adjectives are most likely equal and a comma is needed between the adjectives.

Examples of Equal Adjectives that Require Commas Between them:

small, slow truck   slow, small truck *(Adjectives Reversed)*

No Comma is Needed Between Adjectives that are NOT Equal:

small toy truck   friendly Siamese kitten   ten glass marbles

Examples of Using Commas Between Two "Equal" Adjectives in Sentences:

Last summer, we visited the **sunny, tropical** Fiji Islands.
Last summer, we visited the **tropical, sunny** Fiji Islands.
Adjectives can be reversed, so a comma is needed.

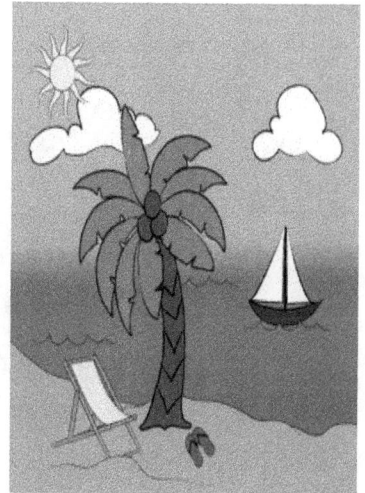

Jena enjoyed the **warm, moist** sea breeze.
Jena enjoyed the **moist, warm** sea breeze.
Adjectives can be reversed, so a comma is needed.

Sailboats drifted over the **choppy, white** waves.
Sailboats drifted over the **white, choppy** waves.
Adjectives can be reversed, so a comma is needed.

Use Commas Between Equal Adjectives

Now You Try!
Correctly place commas between the equal adjectives in four of the sentences below. (Two sentences DO NOT require commas). Then rewrite the four sentences reversing the adjectives. If the sentence flows well, then the adjectives are equal and a comma must be used between them.

Example: Kimberly loved her <u>shiny,</u> <u>new</u> sports car.
Kimberly loved her **new, shiny** sports car. *Adjectives Reversed.*

1. The warm sweet sugar cookies tasted delicious.

   _____

2. Mindy hugged the cuddly tiny kitten.

   _____

3. Sophia shaped the mushy cool clay into round balls.

   _____

4. The wild tree monkey swung from limb to limb.

   _____

5. Rafa finished the adventurous dangerous journey.

   _____

6. Jordan discovered ten copper pennies buried in the sand.

   _____

Write It
Write 2 sentences using equal adjectives to describe exact nouns. Place a comma between the equal adjectives.

1. _____

   _____

2. _____

   _____

14

Adjectives in a Series

Adjectives can be written in a series or list of three or more words. Use commas to separate each adjective. Place a conjunction (and, or) before the last adjective listed.

Examples:

John's pepperoni pizza tasted **hot**, **spicy**, and **cheesy**.

Lewis enjoyed **windy**, **rainy**, or **snowy** weather.

Now You Try!

Place commas in the sentences below to separate the adjectives in a series. Each sentence requires two commas.

Example: The sea breeze felt **cool**, **gentle**, and **moist**.

1. Mina froze as the tall lean shadowy figure approached.

2. The fruit juice tasted cool sweet and refreshing.

3. Our Hawaiian vacation was warm sunny and relaxing.

4. The marathon race was long windy and difficult.

5. The beagle puppy was playful friendly and smart.

6. Maurice's van looked old rusted and worn out.

7. The banana nut bread tasted sweet fresh and nutty.

8. The frightened toddler spoke in a quiet squeaky and shaky voice.

9. The soldiers were brave loyal and ready to fight.

10. Danita's favorite blanket felt soft fluffy and velvety.

Write It

Write 2 sentences using commas to separate adjectives in a series.

1. _____

   _____

2. _____

   _____

Use Sensational Sensory (5 Senses) Words

Use sensational sensory words that appeal to the reader's 5 senses. Help the reader imagine by using words that describe sight, sound, taste, touch, and smell.

Examples:

Sight: teal blue, huge, shiny

Taste: chocolaty, sugary, tart

Touch: bumpy, smooth, piping hot

Sound: bang, boom, buzz, shush

Smell: coffee, pine, garlicky

Examples of Using Sensory Words:

On Saturday, Dino baked an **apple** pie. *(Taste)*

First, he stirred the ingredients in a **large glass mixing bowl.** *(Sight)*

Slowly, he stirred in a cup of **sugar**, **fresh apples**, and a tablespoon of **cinnamon**. *(Taste)*

Next, he poured the **cool, chunky** mixture into a ready-made pie crust. *(Touch)*

Then, he baked the pie for 45 minutes. Before long, the oven sounded a long ***buzzzz!*** *(Sound)*

When he opened the oven door, the smell of **sweet baked apples** and **spicy cinnamon** filled the house. *(Smell)*

We couldn't wait to taste the **sugary, sweet apples** and **fresh, flaky crust**. *(Taste)*

Use Sensational Sensory (5 Senses) Words
Avoid Dull Words and Use Sensational Sensory Words
Sensory Word List

DULL	SIGHT
Colors	Words to Use
black	charcoal, coal, ebony, graphite, jet-black, licorice, midnight black, onyx, pitch-black, slate
blue	aqua, baby blue, blue-green, denim, indigo, light blue, navy blue, peacock blue, royal blue, sapphire, sky blue, teal, turquoise
brown	beige, bronze, brunette, caramel, chestnut, coffee, copper, khaki, mocha, nutmeg, oak, tan, teak, toast, walnut
gray	ash, cloud gray, concrete gray, lead, oyster, shadowy gray, silvery, slate gray, smoky gray, steel, stone
green	apple, avocado, chartreuse, emerald, evergreen, fern, forest green, jade, lime, mint, mossy, sage, seaweed
orange	amber, apricot, bronze, carrot, copper, coral, ginger, light orange, peach, pumpkin, tangerine, terra cotta
pink	coral, dark pink, fuchsia, hot pink, light pink, magenta, mauve
purple	fuchsia, grape, lavender, light purple, lilac, mauve, orchid, periwinkle, plum, violet, violet red, wine
red	berry, blood-red, brick red, candy apple, cherry red, crimson, fiery, magenta, maroon, rose, ruby, scarlet, strawberry, wine
white	alabaster, blond, chalky, chiffon, cream, ghost white, ivory, marshmallow, pearl, snow
yellow	amber, banana, butter, butterscotch, canary, gold, golden, honey, lemon, light yellow, mustard, sunset, topaz
multicolor	brindle, calico, kaleidoscope, rainbow, speckled, tabby
Shades	**Words to Use**
bright	ablaze, aglow, blazing, brilliant, dazzling, fiery, flashing, flickering, gleaming, glimmering, glistening, glittering, glittery, glowing, golden, jeweled, luminous, polished, radiant, shimmering, shiny, sparkling, sparkly, sunny, twinkling
clear	cloudless, crystal, crystal clear, glassy, glossy, luminous, see-through, sheer, translucent, transparent
dull	bleak, blurry, cloudy, dim, dirty, dreary, dusky, faded, gray, hazy, murky, shadowy, sunless

Use Sensational Sensory (5 Senses) Words

Avoid Dull Words and Use Sensational Sensory Words
Sensory Word List

DULL	SIGHT
Sizes	**Words to Use**
big	brawny, burly, colossal, enormous, giant, gigantic, huge, humongous, husky, immense, large, majestic, massive, monstrous, towering, tremendous, vast
heavy	ample, beefy, bulky, chubby, chunky, hefty, huge, massive, obese, overweight, weighty
short	compact, diminutive, dwarfed, little, petite, pint-size, puny, slight, stunted, tiny, undersized
small	bite-size, bitty, dainty, miniature, munchkin, petite, pint-sized, puny, scanty, teensy, teeny, tiny
tall	gigantic, lanky, overgrown, statuesque, sky-high, towering
thin	beanpole, bony, feeble, frail, gaunt, lanky, lean, long-legged, scrawny, skeletal, skinny, slender, slight, stick, trim, twig
Shapes	**Words to Use**
curved shape	ball-shaped, bubble, circular, crescent, cylindrical, disk-shaped, dome-shaped, egg-shaped, elliptical, oval, ring, round, sphere
other	box-shaped, cone-shaped, cube, curved, diamond-shaped, flat, four-sided, heart-shaped, rectangular, square, star-shaped, triangular
Age	**Words to Use**
new	brand-new, cutting edge, fashionable, fresh, modern, state-of-the-art, recent, trendy, unused, up-to-date, young, youthful
old	aged, ancient, antique, broken-down, dated, elderly, feeble, gray-haired, historic, old-fashioned, prehistoric, ragged, run-down, withered, worn, worn-out, wrinkled, wrinkly
Condition	**Words to Use**
clean	bright, flawless, fresh, immaculate, laundered, neat, sparkling, spick-and-span, spotless, uncluttered, unsoiled, untainted, washed, white
dirty	dusty, filthy, greasy, grimy, grubby, messy, muddy, polluted, scummy, slimy, smudged, soiled, sooty, straggly, untidy, unwashed

Use Sensational Sensory (5 Senses) Words
Avoid Dull Words and Use Sensational Sensory Words

SMELL	
Dull	**Words to Use**
bad	burnt, cigarette, decayed, dusty, fishy, mildewed, moldy, musty, rancid, rotten, rotten eggs, salty, skunky, smoky, sour, spoiled, stinky, swampy, sweaty, vinegary
chemical	alcohol, ammonia, bleach, gasoline, Lysol, oil
floral	carnation, gardenia, honeysuckle, jasmine, lavender, rose
fruit	apple, banana, blueberry, cherry, citrus, fruity, lemony, mango, orange, peach, raspberry, strawberry, watermelon
good	buttery, candied, candy apple, caramel, cherry, chocolaty, citrus, cocoa, coconut, coffee, cotton candied, fragrant, fresh, honey, lemony, minty, peppermint, perfumed, piney, pine tree, soapy, sugary, sweet, toasted, toffee, vanilla-scented
spiced	barbecued, cinnamon, curry, garlicky, ginger, peppery, salty, seasoned, spicy, spicy pumpkin

SOUND	
loud	bang, beep, boo, boom, bong, burst, buzz, chime, clang, clank, clatter, click, clink, clip-clop, crack, crackle, crash, crunch, cry, ding, ding-dong, howl, giggle, jangle, jingle, knock, moan, plop, pop, pow, rat-a-tat, rattle, ring, roar, rumble, scream, screech, shout, shriek, siren, slurp, smash, snap, snore, spurt, stomp, tap, thud, thump, toot, vroom, wail, weep, whack, wham, whine, whistle, whoop, zap, zoom
soft	breathless, burp, buzz, click, creak, drip, fizz, gasp, hiss, hum, hushed, mumble, phew, pitter-patter, purr, rip, rustle, sigh, sizzle, swish, tick-tock, whimper, whir, whisk, whisper, whiz, zip
animal	arff, baa, bark, bray, buzz, chatter, cheap, chirp, cluck, coo, croak, cuckoo, eek, err, gobble, growl, hee-haw, hiss, honk, hoot, howl, hum, meow, mew, moo, neigh, oink, peep, purr, quack, rarr, rattle, ribbit, roar, snarl, snort, squawk, squeak, squeal, tu-whoo, tweet, warble, whinny, whistle, yap, yelp, yip

Use Sensational Sensory (5 Senses) Words
Avoid Dull Words and Use Sensational Sensory Words

TASTE	
Dull	**Words to Use**
bad	bitter, bland, burnt, curdled, fishy, flat, flavorless, greasy, lemony, limey, moldy, oily, rancid, rotten, sour, spoiled, tangy, tart, tasteless, unflavored, unseasoned, vinegary
fruit	apple, apricot, banana, citrus, fruity, lemony, orange, peach, strawberry, watermelon
good	buttery, candied, candy apple, caramel, cherry, chocolaty, citrus, cocoa, coffee, cotton candied, creamy, crisp, crispy, crunchy, flaky, fresh, honey, lemony, maple, minty, nutty, peppermint, sugary, sweet, toasted, toffee, vanilla
nuts	almond, coconut, hazelnut, peanut, pecan, walnut
spiced	barbecued, cinnamon, curry, garlicky, ginger-spiced, hot, peppery, salty, sautéed, seasoned, spicy, spicy pumpkin, well-seasoned
TOUCH	
cold	arctic, bitter, brisk, chilly, cool, crisp, frigid, frosty, frozen, ice-cold, icy, nippy, refreshing, snowy, wintry
hard	crispy, crunchy, dense, firm, frozen, inflexible, rigid, rocklike, solid, stiff, stiff as a board
heavy	beefy, bulky, chunky, hefty, loaded, massive, thick, weighty
hot	baking, blazing, blistering, boiling, broiling, burning, flaming, lukewarm, piping-hot, roasting, scorching, sizzling, smoldering, steaming, sweltering, tepid, toasty, torrid, tropical
light	airy, buoyant, featherweight, feathery, lightweight, weightless
rough	bumpy, choppy, coarse, craggy, crumbling, grainy, gritty, jagged, knotty, lumpy, prickly, ragged, rickety, rocky, sandy, scratchy, uneven
sharp	jagged, knifelike, pierced, pointy, prickly, razor-sharp, sharp-edged, spiky, thorny
soft	brittle, creamy, cushioned, delicate, doughy, feathery, flimsy, fluffy, furry, mushy, padded, silky, snuggly, spongy, squishy, velvety
wet	damp, humid, misty, moist, rainy, slimy, slushy, soaked, soggy, sticky, sweaty, waterlogged, watery

Use Sensational Sensory (5 Senses) Words

Now You Try!

Complete each sentence below by adding a sensory word. Use the *Sensory Word List* on pages 17-20 if you need help. When writing sound words, italicize or tilt letters to the right to emphasize the sound word.

Example: Tyra jumped off the slide and landed with a *thump*!

(Sound)

1. Lara watched the _____ meteor plummet toward Earth.

(Sight)

2. The _____ balloons were filled with helium.

(Sight)

3. The _____ smell of the pepperoni pizza filled the room.

(Smell)

4. Ben emptied the _____ garbage.

(Smell)

5. The mini-van crashed into the building with a loud _____.

(Sound)

6. Tyler felt the baseball _____ over his head.

(Sound)

7. Tammy baked _____ breakfast biscuits.

(Taste)

8. The Oreo cookie tasted _____ and _____ .

(Taste)   (Taste)

9. Helen sipped on the _____ strawberry milkshake.

(Touch)

10. Mia pressed the _____ bread dough into a pan.

(Touch)

Write It

Write two sentences using sensory (5 senses) words.

1. _____

_____

2. _____

_____

Use Sizzling Sound Words

Use sizzling sound words to increase sensory details. When writing sound words, italicize words (tilt letters to the right) so readers will say the word with emphasis or expression.

Examples: *BOOM! Crash! Whack! Pop!*

Notice in the passages below how the authors use italicizing, exclamation points, repetition (repeating words), and capitalization to vary the emphasis or expression placed on the sound words.

Examples of Using Sound Words in Sentences:

CRASH! The stained glass ceiling splintered in a ruin of multicolored shards, and Festus the bronze dragon dropped into the department store.

The dragon clicked. Long *creak.* Two short *clicks. Creak. Creak. Bang!* Jason found himself flat on his back.

> Rick Riordan, *The Heroes of Olympus: The Lost Hero*

I slammed my forehead right into the top of the doorframe. *Wham!*

> Jennifer Cervantes, *Tortilla Sun*

BAM!

SOUND WORD LIST	
loud	bam, bang, beep, bong, boo, boom, burst, buzz, clang, clank, clap, clatter, click, clink, clip-clop, crack, crackle, crash, crunch, cry, ding, ding-dong, giggle, honk, howl, knock, moan, plop, pop, pow, rat-a-tat, ring, roar, rumble, scream, screech, scrunch, shout, shriek, siren, slurp, smash, snap, snore, splat, spurt, sputter, stomp, tap, thud, thump, toot, vroom, v-room, wail, weep, whack, wham, whine, whip, whir, whistle, whoop, whop, zap, zoom
soft	burp, buzz, chime, click, creak, drip, fizz, gasp, hiss, hum, hushed, jingle, jingling, mumble, phew, pitter-patter, ping, purr, rattle, rip, rippling, rustle, shh, shush, sigh, sizzle, snip, splash, squish, swish, swoosh, tick, tick-tock, wheeze, whimper, whisper, whiz, whoosh, zip

Use Sizzling Sound Words

Now You Try!
Complete each sentence below by adding a sound word for emphasis. When writing sound words, italicize (tilt letters to the right) the sound word. Try using repetition or uppercase letters to emphasize sounds and lower case letters for less emphasis. Use the *Sound Word List* on page 22 if you need help.

Example: Tara kicked the soccer ball with a fierce *WHACK!*

1. Aliyah tiptoed across the wooden floor. _____ , _____ .

2. Lorenzo hopped off the slide and landed with a _____ !

3. Tam heard the _____ , _____ , _____ of popcorn.

4. _____ ! The motorcycle collided with the mini-van.

5. The _____ of the airplane engine could be heard above us.

6. The red sports car _____ as it rounded the corner.

7. Grandma's old lawn mower started with a _____ .

8. The _____ of rain drops woke Giselle up.

9. Marcy could hear the _____ of coins in her change purse.

10. The _____ of thunder could be heard for miles.

Write It
Write two sentences using sound words. Italicize or tilt the letters of the sound words to the right. Try using upper case letters, repetition, and exclamation points for more emphasis.

1. _____

_____

2. _____

_____

Use Audacious Animal Sound Words

Use audacious animal sound words. When an animal makes a communication sound, write it as dialogue. Place quotation marks around the sound words and the end dialogue punctuation. The first letter of the first word in the dialogue will be upper case. Use interesting animal dialogue tags.

Examples: arff, bark, meow, neigh, oink, woof

Examples of Using Animal Sound Words and Dialogue Tags in Sentences:

"Quack, quack, quack," **squawked** the duck, flapping its wings.

The night owl **hooted,** "Tu-whoo, tu-whoo."

The bulldog **barked** loudly, "Arf, arf, arf."

Arf!!
Woof!
Errr...
Ruff!

	ANIMAL SOUNDS AND DIALOGUE TAGS WORD LIST
Animal Sounds	arf, baa, bark, bray, buzz, ca-caw, chatter, cheep, chirp, chirrup, cluck, cock-a-doodle-doo, coo, croak, cuckoo, eek, err, gobble, growl, hee-haw, hiss, honk, hoo-hoo, hoot, howl, hum, meow, me-ow, moo, neigh, oink, peep, purr, quack, rarr, rattle, ribbit, roar, ruff, snarl, snort, squawk, squeak, squeal, ssss, tu-whoo, tweet, warble, whinny, whistle, woof, yap, yelp, yip, yowl, zzzz
Animal Dialogue Tags	barked, brayed, bumbled, buzzed, cackled, cawed, chattered, cheeped, chirped, clucked, cooed, cried, croaked, crooned, crowed, gobbled, growled, grunted, hissed, honked, hooted, howled, hummed, mewed, mooed, neighed, panted, purred, roared, sang, shrieked, snarled, snorted, squeaked, squealed, squawked, tooted, trilled, tweeted, wallowed, warbled, whined, whinnied, whistled, woofed, yapped, yelped

Use Audacious Animal Sound Words

Now You Try!

Place animal sound words and end sentence punctuation in each sentence below. Place quotation marks around the animal sound words and end sentence punctuation. Use repetition as needed. Use the *Animal Sounds* and *Dialogue Tags Word List* on page 24 if you need help.

Example: Bailey, my pet hen, chased me squawking, "Cluck, cluck, cluck!"

1. The poodle puppy barked, _____

2. The angry lion snarled, _____

3. The squirrel scurried up the tree squealing, _____

4. Wilbur, the hungry pig, snorted, _____

5. The baby bluebird chirped, _____

6. The gray horse snorted a loud, _____

7. The bumpy bullfrog croaked, _____

8. The rooster greeted the day with a loud, _____

9. The rattlesnake gave a long and low warning, _____

10. The Siamese kitten mewed, _____

Write It

Write 2 sentences with animal sound words and interesting animal dialogue tags. Place quotation marks around the animal sounds and end sentence punctuation. Use the *Animal Sounds and Dialogue Tags Word List* on page 24 if you need help.

1. _____

   _____

2. _____

   _____

Use Repetition! Yes! Yes! Yes!

Use repetitive words (repeating words) and phrases for emphasis. Repeating words can help emphasize a point, provide humor, or create a dramatic effect.

Example: Please, please, please! Please let me go to the game!

Examples of Using Repetition in Sentences:

"Move it, move it, move it!" instructed Ripred, herding them all from the open bank and into a tunnel.

Suzanne Collin, *Gregor the Overlander*

"Nicely done, nicely done!" cried the goose. "Try it again, try it again!"

E.B. White, *Charlotte's Web*

"Won't, won't, won't, WON'T!" J.K. Rowling, *Harry Potter and the Half-Blood Prince*

Now You Try!

Add repetitive words to each sentence below.

Example: "Go faster!" shrieked Sue, "Faster, faster, _faster!_"

1. Go get help! Go! Go! Go! _____ !

2. Never! Never! _____ in a hundred years!

3. We discovered gold! Gold! Precious _____ !

4. We're rich! We're rich! Rich! Rich! _____ !

5. I said no! No, no, _____ !

6. Well done! Well done! _____ !

7. The lights flickered on. Off. On. _____ . _____. _____.

Write It

Write 2 sentences using repetition to emphasize a point, provide humor, or create a dramatic effect. Place appropriate punctuation.

1. _____

   _____

2. _____

   _____

Use Exact Vivid Verbs

Action verbs are words that describe the action in the sentence. Avoid dull, general verbs by using exact, vivid action verbs that create a picture in the reader's mind.

Examples:

Avoid Dull/General Verbs	Use Exact Vivid Action Verbs
ate	devoured, gobbled, nibbled
got	bought, found, obtained
made	baked, built, constructed
ran	jogged, raced, sprinted
saw	glanced, stared, watched
went	biked, drove, skated

Examples of Replacing Dull Verbs with Exact Vivid Action Verbs:

Manny **went** to the soccer game. *Went is dull and general.*
Manny **drove** to the soccer game. *Drove is specific.*

The soccer player **ran** toward the goal. *Ran is dull.*
The soccer player **sprinted** toward the goal. *Sprinted is livelier.*

Manny **saw** the soccer players **go** up and down the field.
Saw and go are dull.
Manny **watched** as the soccer players **raced** up and down
the field. *Watched and raced are livelier.*

The soccer player **made** a goal. *Made is dull and general.*
The soccer player **flipped** on his back and **kicked**
the ball in the goal. *Flipped and kicked are livelier and more exact.*

Use Exact Vivid Verbs
Avoid Dull Verbs and Use Exact Vivid Action Verbs

EXACT ACTION VERB WORD LIST	
Dull	**Words to Use**
ate	chewed, consumed, devoured, gobbled, gorged, grazed, inhaled, licked, munched, nibbled, picked at, snacked on, stuffed, wolfed
blew up	blasted, burst, demolished, detonated, erupted, exploded, gushed, ruptured, thundered
broke	busted, cracked, crumbled, crushed, destroyed, fractured, severed, shattered, smashed, snapped, split, splintered
bump into	banged, collided, crashed, crunched, jerked, knocked, pounded, sacked, slammed, smacked, smashed, wrecked
came	appeared, approached, arrived, entered, landed, reached, visited
climbed	ascended, crawled, hiked up, mounted, rose, scaled, soared, trekked
covered	bandaged, blanketed, buried, camouflaged, carpeted, concealed, draped, enveloped, hid, shaded, veiled, wrapped
cried	bawled, groaned, growled, howled, moaned, sniveled, sobbed, wailed, wept, whined
cut	carved, chopped, clipped, diced, hacked, sliced, slit, snipped
did	accomplished, achieved, attained, carried out, completed, concluded, ended, finished, fulfilled, wrapped up
drank	chugged, gulped, guzzled, sipped, slurped, swallowed, swigged
fell	dropped, flipped, plummeted, plunged, stumbled, toppled, tripped, tumbled
fixed	mended, patched, rebuilt, reconstructed, repaired, revised
flew	circled, dove, drifted, floated, fluttered, glided, hovered, rocketed, shot, soared, streaked, swooped, whooshed, zoomed
fought	battled, boxed, brawled, clashed, dueled, feuded, quarreled, sparred, struggled, wrestled
found	acquired, detected, discovered, explored, investigated, located, probed, pursued, recovered, researched, spotted, uncovered

Use Exact Vivid Verbs
Avoid Dull Verbs and Use Exact Vivid Action Verbs

EXACT ACTION VERB WORD LIST	
Dull	**Words to Use**
gave	awarded, bestowed, delivered, donated, gifted, granted, handed, offered, presented, provided, won
got	accepted, achieved, attained, awarded, bought, caught, chose, collected, discovered, earned, found, grabbed, obtained, purchased, received, snatched, won
grew	enlarged, expanded, increased, rose, shot up, sprouted, stretched
held	clasped, clenched, clutched, cradled, cuddled, embraced, grabbed, grasped, gripped, hugged, squeezed
hit	bashed, clobbered, clocked, crushed, knocked, pelted, pounded, pummeled, punched, shattered, slugged, smacked, smashed, whacked
hung	dangled, drooped, hooked, suspended
jumped	bolted, bounced, dove, flipped, hopped, hurdled, launched, leapt, lunged, lurched, parachuted, plummeted, plunged, pounced, skipped, sprang, tripped, vaulted
leave/left	abandoned, departed, deserted, disappeared, escaped, fled, vanished, withdrew
liked	admired, adored, appreciated, cherished, desired, devoted, enjoyed, favored, fond of, loved, respected, treasured
looked	admired, examined, gazed, glanced, glared, glimpsed, inspected, noted, noticed, peered, observed, searched, spotted, stared, studied, surveyed, watched, witnessed
made	assembled, baked, built, constructed, cooked, created, designed, developed, drew, fashioned, formed, invented, manufactured, produced, scored, shaped
pulled	dragged, hauled, jerked, lugged, towed, tugged, yanked
pushed	jolted, nudged, poked, pressed, prodded, propelled, shoved, thrusted

Use Exact Vivid Verbs
Avoid Dull Verbs and Use Exact Vivid Action Verbs

EXACT ACTION VERB WORD LIST	
Dull	**Words to Use**
put	deposited, embedded, inserted, installed, placed, set
ran	bolted, chased, darted, dashed, escaped, galloped, hurried, hustled, jogged, raced, scampered, scrambled, scurried, sprinted, streaked, trotted
see/saw	gazed, glanced, glared, glimpsed, inspected, noted, noticed, peered, observed, spotted, stared, studied, surveyed, watched
stopped	blocked, ceased, concluded, discontinued, halted, obstructed, quit, restrained, terminated
thought	believed, considered, hoped, imagined, pondered, reflected
threw	flipped, flung, hurled, launched, lobbed, pelted, pitched, tossed
told	advised, confessed, educated, explained, expressed, informed, instructed, mentioned, proposed, reported, revealed
took	captured, collected, confiscated, grabbed, grasped, looted, nabbed, obtained, seized, snagged, snatched
tried	attempted, endeavored, experimented, proposed, strived, tested
turned	flipped, pirouetted, pivoted, reeled, rotated, spun, swiveled, twirled, twisted, weaved, whirled, wiggled, zigzagged
walked	ambled, crept, danced, drifted, hiked, hobbled, journeyed, limped, lurked, marched, meandered, paced, paraded, pranced, roamed, sauntered, shuffled, skipped, stepped, stomped, strolled, strutted, tiptoed, trekked, trudged, waddled, waltzed, wandered
wanted	chose, craved, desired, longed for, needed, prayed for, required, wished, yearned
went	biked, bused, cabbed, crawled, cruised, departed, drove, escaped, flew, hopped, journeyed, moved, raced, rolled, skated, skipped, sped, travelled, traversed, Uberred, visited, walked

Use Exact Vivid Verbs

Now You Try!

Write an exact vivid action verb to replace the word written below the line. Use the *Exact Action Verb Word List* on pages 28-30 if you need help.

Example: Veronica <u>slurped</u> the cold apple juice.
             (Drank)

1. Abraham _____ a chocolate chip cake.
             (Made)

2. Jane _____ to the supermarket to buy groceries.
          (Went)

3. Jason _____ a gold medal for winning the race.
         (Got)

4. The toddler grabbed the plastic rattle and _____ it.
          (Threw)

5. Mrs. Martell _____ at the student and smiled.
        (Looked)

6. The thief _____ the woman's purse and sprinted away.
        (Took)

7. The eagle _____ above the snowy mountains.
        (Flew)

8. Mariel quickly _____ the pumpkin pie.
        (Ate)

9. Julio _____ the hot chocolate.
       (Drank)

10. Adam _____ his homework assignment.
       (Did)

Write It

Write 2 sentences using an exact action verb.

1. _____

   _____

2. _____

   _____

Use Replacement Words for Said

Use replacement words for *said* when writing dialogue (the exact words spoken). *Said* is boring and can be replaced with words that are livelier and more descriptive.

Examples of Using Replacement Words for Said in Sentences:

"I have to go home and finish my homework," Rylan **said**.
"I have to go home and finish my homework," Rylan **groaned**.

"Hurry up!" Owen **said**. "Run faster!"
"Hurry up!" Owen **yelled**. "Run faster!"

"I lost my wallet at the mall today!" Elena **said**.
"I lost my wallet at the mall today!" Elena **cried**.

SAID WORD LIST

accused, admitted, advised, agreed, announced, answered, argued, asked, bantered, barked, begged, bellowed, blurted, boasted, bragged, called, cautioned, cheered, choked, chuckled, claimed, commanded, commented, complained, confessed, cried, dared, decided, demanded, divulged, echoed, exclaimed, explained, gasped, groaned, growled, grumbled, grunted, guessed, hissed, hollered, huffed, insisted, interjected, interrupted, joked, mentioned, moaned, mumbled, muttered, noted, objected, observed, ordered, panted, pleaded, prayed, proclaimed, promised, proposed, questioned, quipped, quoted, reasoned, remarked, repeated, replied, reported, roared, scolded, scowled, screamed, shouted, shrieked, sighed, smirked, snapped, snarled, snickered, snorted, sobbed, squealed, stammered, stated, stuttered, suggested, taunted, teased, threatened, urged, uttered, vowed, wailed, warned, wheezed, whimpered, whined, whispered, yelled

Use Replacement Words for Said

Now You Try!
Add a replacement word for "said" to each sentence below. Use the *Said Word List* on page 32 if you need help.

Example: "I love French fries and hamburgers," *exclaimed* Raul.

1. "Have a nice day," Manny _____.

2. Elise _____ , "Does anyone want to play basketball?"

3. The teacher _____ , "Everyone passed the math test!"

4. "Please don't be late," Danita _____.

5. "Jamie, let's go!" Melanie _____.

6. "I'll buy you lunch today," Edwin _____.

7. "Most volunteers work in the morning," Jamal _____.

8. "Leave me alone!" _____ Martina.

9. "Be quite. Karsyn is sleeping," _____ Erin.

10. "I'm hungry!" _____ Leo.

Write It
Write 2 sentences with dialogue using replacement words for *said*. Use the Said Word List on page 32 if you need help.

1. _____

_____

2. _____

_____

Use Awesome Adverbs

Adverbs are words that describe verbs, adjectives, and other adverbs, but their main job is to describe verbs. Adverbs often describe when, where, how, how often, and to what extent an action is happening. They are often placed directly before or after the verb.

Examples of Using Adverbs in Sentences:

Thomas mowed the lawn **yesterday**. *Yesterday tells when.*

He planted flowers **outside** in the garden. *Outside tells where.*

A calico cat **quietly** watched. *Quietly tells how.*

He **always** gardens on Saturdays. *Always tells how often.*

Thomas **almost** fell off the ladder. *Almost tells to what extent.*

CATEGORY	ADVERB WORD LIST
When	afternoon, always, annually, before, daily, early, last year, later, monthly, now, recently, soon, today, tomorrow, tonight, weekly, yearly, yesterday
Where	above, anywhere, around, behind, below, down, downstairs, everywhere, here, indoors, inside, outside, somewhere, there, under, up, upstairs
How	abruptly, affectionately, angrily, anxiously, artistically, bashfully, bitterly, boldly, bravely, brutally, calmly, carelessly, caringly, casually, cautiously, cheerfully, cleverly, clumsily, coldly, constantly, cowardly, courageously, daringly, decisively, delicately, eagerly, effortlessly, elegantly, faithfully, fearlessly, fiercely, fondly, frantically, gallantly, gently, gracefully, happily, heroically, honestly, hopefully, humbly, jokingly, joyfully, lazily, loudly, mildly, nervously, oddly, patiently, peacefully, playfully, politely, powerfully, quietly, radiantly, recklessly, repeatedly, rudely, sadly, savagely, shakily, shockingly, shyly, simply, sincerely, skillfully, sleepily, slowly, slyly, smoothly, sneakily, speedily, steadily, strangely, strongly, stunningly, sweetly, timidly, tirelessly, tragically, truly, truthfully, valiantly, viciously, weakly, wickedly, wildly, wearily, willfully, wisely, worriedly
How Often	always, frequently, often, never, rarely, seldom, sometimes
To What Extent	almost, completely, enormously, extremely, greatly, perfectly, really, too, totally, very

Use Awesome Adverbs

Now You Try!
Place an adverb in each sentence below. Use the *Adverb Word List* on page 34 if you need help.

1. _____ , the mountain climbers ascended Mt. Everest. **(When)**

2. Avery finished the vacuuming _____. **(Where)**

3. Mona _____ watched the clown enter the room. **(How)**

4. Karina _____ sipped the delicious fruit juice. **(How)**

5. _____ , Ramona climbed into the tree house. **(When)**

6. The tiny yellow duck _____ paddled across the lake. **(How)**

7. The softball team _____ plays on Sundays. **(How often)**

8. Greg _____ finished his homework. **(To what extent)**

9. _____ , we start our first day of school. **(When)**

10. Marissa _____ finishes her homework on time. **(How often)**

Write It
Write 2 sentences using adverbs to describe verbs.

1. _____

_____

2. _____

_____

Introductory Adverbs

Introductory adverbs can be placed in the beginning of sentences to help describe the main clause or sentence that follows. Use a comma after introductory adverbs.

Examples of Introductory Adverbs in Sentences:

Yesterday, Juanita painted a ceramic flower vase.
Patiently, she waited for the paint to dry.

Now You Try!
Rewrite each sentence below moving the highlighted adverb to the beginning of the sentence. Place a comma after the adverb.

Example: Manny **carefully** rode his mountain bike down the steep hill.
Carefully, Manny rode his mountain bike down the steep hill.

1. The rescuers **daringly** climbed the steep cliff.

   _____

2. Enrique finished the gardening **yesterday**.

   _____

3. Kayla **cautiously** helped the elderly man cross the street.

   _____

4. Jonah **quietly** read the last few chapters of *Black Beauty*.

   _____

5. David **slowly** limped off the soccer field.

   _____

6. Kim **gently** lifted the crying baby from the crib.

   _____

7. Jayden **bravely** dove off of the sinking boat into the freezing lake.

   _____

Use Location Words

Use location words to describe where events are happening. Location words help the reader imagine the location of the events.

Examples of location words: above, across, around, behind, below, beside, between, bottom, down, downstairs, front, inside, left, middle, on top, out, outside, over, right, top, under, up, upside down, upstairs

Examples of Using Location Words in Sentences:

Cathy raced **up** the stairs. When she reached the **top**, she turned **right** and sprinted **across** the living room.

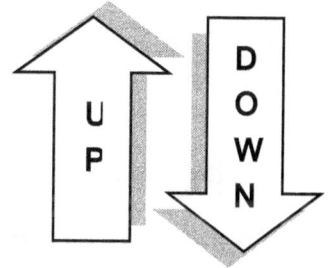

Now You Try!

Add location words to each sentence below.

Example: The brown mouse scurried _up_ the fence.

1. Brandon held the tennis racket _____ his head.

2. Brutus buried his dog bone _____ the oak tree.

3. The jet soared high _____ our heads.

4. Dion trotted _____ the track field.

5. Mom raced _____ when she heard the tires screech.

6. A gray poodle puppy darted _____ the street.

7. Marta tossed her tennis shoes _____ the table.

Write It

Write 2 sentences using location words.

1. _____

_____

2. _____

_____

Use Incredible Interjections

Interjections are words that express strong feeling or emotion. Use incredible interjections to make sentences more interesting. Strong interjections are followed by an exclamation point. Interjections can also be followed by a comma, period, or question mark.

Examples: Wow!   Really?   No.   Well, I guess so.

Examples of Using Interjections in Sentences:

"Hurray!" exclaimed Johnny. "We won!"

"Really?" asked Monica.

"Yes, we won!" answered Johnny.

"Wow! Congratulations!" replied Monica.

"Thanks," responded Johnny.

INTERJECTION WORD LIST

ah, aha, aloha, alright, awesome, bingo, blah, boo, bravo, bummer, bye, cheers, congratulations, cool, eek, eh, fabulous, fantastic, golly, good, good job, goodbye, good morning, gosh, great, great job, ha, ha-ha, hello, hey, hi, huh, hum, hurray, marvelous, maybe, no, no way, oh, oh my, oh no, oh well, okay, oops, ouch, phew, please, really, right, sure, thanks, uh-huh, uh-oh, um, way to go, well, whew, whoa, wonderful, wow, yah, yahoo, yeah, yep, yes, yikes, yippee

Use Incredible Interjections

Now You Try!
Add an interjection to each sentence below. Use the Interjection Word List on page 38 if you need help.

Example: _Hey_, what's the big idea? asked Chip.

1. _____! Let's go swimming today.

2. _____ , we can all go to the movies.

3. What did you say, _____?

4. _____! I can't play because I have to finish my homework.

5. _____? Why do you think that?

6. _____ , I don't want to go shopping right now.

7. _____! That was the best banana milkshake.

8. _____ , you won the spelling bee!

9. I just can't believe what happen. _____!

10. _____ . What do you want to do today?

Write It
Write 2 sentences using interjections. Interjections may be followed by a comma, period, question mark, or exclamation point.

1. _____

_____

2. _____

_____

Use Super Synonyms

Synonyms are words that have the same or similar meaning. Good writers replace dull, overused words with interesting synonyms. Use a thesaurus or www.thesaurus.com to find synonyms.

Example: ran (dull and overused). Try **raced** or **sprinted** instead.

Examples of Replacing Dull, Overused Words with Interesting Synonyms:

Nick **hit** the baseball over the fence and **ran** around the bases. *Hit* and *ran* are dull and overused.

Nick **smacked** the baseball over the fence and **trotted** around the bases. *(Smacked and trotted are more interesting).*

EXAMPLES OF USING INTERESTING SYNONYMS
(USE ALL OF THE WORD LISTS IN THIS BOOK FOR MORE SYNONYMS)

Dull	More Interesting	Dull	More Interesting
afraid	fearful, terrified	liked	adored, loved
ate	gobbled, inhaled	looked	examined, watched
bad	evil, naughty	nice	kind, friendly
big	enormous, huge	old	aged, worn
found	discovered, spotted	made	built, constructed
good	awesome, great	new	modern, trendy
got	acquired, bought	noise	roared, boom
happy	thrilled, excited	ran	jogged, sprinted
hit	punched, whacked	walked	strolled, tiptoed

Use Super Synonyms

Now You Try!

Replace the dull, overused word listed at the end of each sentence below with an interesting synonym. Use the Synonym Word List on page 40 or the word lists throughout this book if you need help.

Example: Mom _baked_ peanut butter cookies. (Made)

1. Sarah _____ across the dance floor. (Walked)

2. Lori _____ around the track two times. (Ran)

3. Mina _____ her new poodle puppy. (Liked)

4. Gerard _____ the punching bag as hard as he could. (Hit)

5. The doctor _____ the injury on the teenager's leg. (Looked)

6. Jose was _____ about his report card. (Happy)

7. The _____ jacket was falling apart. (Old)

8. The _____ elephant lived in the jungle. (Big)

9. Melinda _____ the chocolate chip cookies. (Ate)

10. Katie _____ a buried treasure in the sand. (Found)

Read the passage below and cross out the dull words in bold print and replace them with interesting synonyms. Use the word lists in this book if you need help.

Jana **went to** the zoo on Friday. First, she **went** over to see the jungle animals. There was a **big** elephant name Jumbo and a **big** giraffe named Ella. She **looked** while Jumbo **ate** grass and Ella **ate** tree leaves. When the animals **saw** Jana, both **went** over to the fence and **looked** at her. Jana wondered if they **wanted** the chocolate candy bar she was **eating**. Before Jana could **put** the candy bar in her purse, Jumbo **took** it with his trunk and **gave** it to Ella.

Use Outstanding Antonyms

Antonyms are words that are opposites. They can be used in sentences and paragraphs to create a contrast or opposite picture in the reader's mind.

Examples: huge *tiny*   fast *slow*   rich *poor*   icy *hot*

Examples of Using Antonyms in Sentences to Create a Contrast or Opposite:

The **fat, black** cat chased the **tiny, white** mouse.

The orange tasted **sweet,** but the lemon tasted **tart.**

It was **cold** and **rainy** on Tuesday, but on Wednesday the weather was **hot** and **sunny.**

HOT   COLD

EXAMPLES OF ANTONYMS			
Word	Antonym (Opposite)	Word	Antonym (Opposite)
active	lazy	poor	rich, wealthy
clean	dirty	rainy	sunny
cool	boiling, piping-hot	same	different
dry	soaked, wet	shout	whisper
empty	full	slow	speedy
gobbled	nibbled	soft	hard
happy	sad, unhappy	sugary	tart, sour
hopeful	hopeless	tall	short
icy	warm, tropical	thrilled	heartbroken
neat	messy	tiny	huge, enormous
never	always	walked	sprinted, raced
old	brand-new	white	black

Use Outstanding Antonyms

Now You Try!
Add antonyms for the bolded word in each sentence below to create a contrast or opposite. Use the antonyms on page 42 if you need help.

Example: The **tiny** woman's husband _towered_ over her.

1. Sumi's room was **clean**, but Jocelynn's room was _____.

2. Juan loves **piping-hot** chocolate, but Maria prefers _____ tea.

3. Polar bears like **cool** temperatures while camels live in _____ climates.

4. Janet quickly **sped** around the _____ moving truck.

5. The elephant was **huge**, but the mouse was _____.

6. The lime was **bitter**, but the strawberries were _____.

7. Kyra's parents were **rich**, but Megan's family was _____.

8. Jayden liked to stay **active** while Max was often _____.

9. Maria spoke in a **whisper**, but Dina _____.

10. Nina **gobbled** the fruit cake while Maya _____ on the grapes.

Write It
Write 2 sentences using antonyms to create a contrast or opposite.

1. _____

_____

2. _____

_____

Use Time Order Words

Time order words tell the reader when events occur. Use introductory time order words to introduce the main sentence, provide smooth transitions, and move the narrative along. Place a comma after introductory time order words.

Examples of Using Introductory Time Order Words:

On Sunday, Janelle baked a chocolate cake.

First, she poured all the ingredients into a bowl.

Then, she blended the mixture for five minutes.

Next, she poured the chocolaty batter into a cake pan and baked it for thirty minutes. **When the timer *buzzed*,** she removed the cake from the oven.

Once upon a time...

TIME ORDER WORD LIST

Time Order Words

after, before, during, earlier, eventually, finally, first, frequently, last, later, meanwhile, momentarily, next, now, occasionally, often, once, previously, second, simultaneously, since, sometimes, soon, suddenly, then, today, tomorrow, when, while, yesterday

Time Order Phrases

after a few days, after a long time, after a while, after several days, after that, all at once, as soon as, at last, at midnight, at sunrise, at sunset, at the end of the day, at times, before long, before school, during spring break, earlier that day, in the beginning, in the morning, last summer, last year, later on, later that day, many years ago, moments later, on Tuesday evening, once upon a time, shortly after, soon after, years ago, when several days had passed

Use Time Order Words

Now You Try!
Place a comma after the time order words in each sentence below.

Example: **At last,** Tina found her lost car keys.

1. Finally Corey worked his way to the front of the lunch line.

2. Before long Jamison reached the top of the huge hill.

3. After a long wait Ming decided to walk home.

4. First we have to press the cookie dough onto the baking sheet.

5. Meanwhile Justin will play guitar while he waits.

6. At times Wanda wondered if she should give up.

7. Shortly after sunrise the rooster crowed.

8. Soon it was time to leave for school.

9. At midnight the grandfather clock *chimed.*

10. When the school year ended the students celebrated their graduation.

Write It
Write 2 sentences using introductory time order words or phrases. Place a comma after the introductory time order words.

1. _____

   _____

2. _____

   _____

Review: Writing Words that Wow!

Directions: Use all of the word skills you've learned to write a 3-4 paragraph personal narrative. Indent each new paragraph. Use the checklist on the writing paper below to ensure you use as many of the word skills as possible.

> Topic: The best day of your life.
> Use one of these story starters to begin your story if you need help getting started.
> Without a doubt, the best day of my life was...
> Can you remember the best day of your life? Well, I can! It was when...

Title: _____

I USED:

☐ EXACT NOUNS

☐ AMAZING ADJECTIVES

☐ EQUAL ADJECTIVES

☐ SENSORY WORDS

☐ SIZZLING SOUND WORDS

☐ ANIMAL SOUND WORDS

☐ REPETITION. YES! YES!

☐ EXACT VIVID VERBS

☐ SAID SYNONYMS

☐ AWESOME ADVERBS

☐ INTRODUCTORY ADVERBS

☐ LOCATION WORDS

☐ INTERJECTIONS

☐ SUPER SYNONYMS

☐ ANTONYMS

☐ TIME ORDER WORDS

Review: Writing Words that Wow!

_____

_____

_____

_____

_____

_____

_____

_____

_____

_____

_____

_____

_____

_____

_____

_____

_____

_____

Review: Writing Words that Wow!

Writing Words that Wow! Checklist

USE THIS CHECKLIST TO EDIT YOUR WRITING

- [ ] USE EXACT NOUNS

- [ ] USE AMAZING ADJECTIVES TO DESCRIBE NOUNS

- [ ] USE EQUAL ADJECTIVES TO DESCRIBE NOUNS

- [ ] USE SENSATIONAL SENSORY (5 SENSES) WORDS

- [ ] USE SIZZLING SOUND WORDS

- [ ] USE AUDACIOUS ANIMAL SOUND WORDS

- [ ] USE REPETITION. YES! YES! YES!

- [ ] USE EXACT VIVID ACTION VERBS

- [ ] USE REPLACEMENT WORDS FOR SAID

- [ ] USE AWESOME ADVERBS

- [ ] USE INTRODUCTORY ADVERBS

- [ ] USE LOCATION WORDS

- [ ] USE INCREDIBLE INTERJECTIONS

- [ ] USE SUPER SYNONYMS

- [ ] USE OUTSTANDING ANTONYMS

- [ ] USE TIME ORDER WORDS

Answer Key

Page 6 (Any appropriate exact noun will work. See the Exact Noun Word List on pages 3-5)

1. I love to eat _lasagna_ for dinner. **(Food)**
2. Tia watched the _ladybug_ land on the grass. **(Insect)**
3. The _princess_ wore a diamond crown to the ball. **(Girl)**
4. The _lion_ roared loudly. **(Animal)**
5. Fran sped down the highway in her _BMW convertible_. **(Car)**
6. Manny gave Danielle a beautiful _rose_. **(Flower)**
7. Ben used a _hammer_ to build a new dog house. **(Tool)**
8. Sarina bought a _Siamese kitten_ at the local pet store. **(Cat)**
9. Chad enjoys playing _football._ **(Sport)**
10. The hospital was filled with many _patients_. **(People)**

Page 12 (Any appropriate adjective will work. See the Adjective Word List on pages 8-11)

1. The ocean waves crashed onto the _sandy_ beach.
2. Tia felt _overjoyed_ when she won the spelling bee.
3. The queen wore a _diamond_ crown on her head.
4. Marisa held the _furry_ kitten in her lap.
5. Edison licked the _sticky_ candy cane.
6. Jennifer baked _fresh_ chocolate chip cookies.
7. Rosa watched the _golden_ sun rise over the hills.
8. The princess wore a _silk_ gown to the ball.
9. The _wild_ kangaroo hopped toward the tourist.
10. Evan carefully climbed up the _rocky_ cliff.

Page 14

1. The warm, sweet sugar cookies tasted delicious.
   The **sweet, warm** sugar cookies tasted delicious.
2. Mindy hugged the cuddly, tiny kitten.
   Mindy hugged the **tiny, cuddly** kitten.
3. Sophia shaped the mushy, cool clay into round balls.
   Sophia shaped the **cool, mushy** clay into round balls.
4. The **wild tree** monkey swung from limb to limb. (No comma needed)
5. Rafa finished the adventurous, dangerous journey.
   Rafa finished the **dangerous, adventurous** journey.
6. Jordan discovered **ten copper** pennies buried in the sand. (No comma needed)

Page 15

1. Mina froze as the tall, lean, shadowy figure approached.
2. The fruit juice tasted cool, sweet, and refreshing.
3. Our Hawaiian vacation was warm, sunny, and relaxing.
4. The marathon race was long, windy, and difficult.
5. The beagle puppy was playful, friendly, and smart.
6. Maurice's van looked old, rusted, and worn out.
7. The banana nut bread tasted sweet, fresh, and nutty.
8. The frightened toddler spoke in a quiet, squeaky, and shaky voice.
9. The soldiers were brave, loyal, and ready to fight.
10. Danita's favorite blanket felt soft, fluffy, and velvety.

50

Answer Key

Page 21 (Any appropriate Sensory Word will work. See the Sensory Word List on pages 17-20)

1. Lara watched the _flickering_ meteor plummet toward Earth. (Sight)
2. The _rainbow colored_ balloons were filled with helium. **(Sight)**
3. The _spicy_ smell of pepperoni pizza filled the room. **(Smell)**
4. Ben emptied the _stinky_ garbage. **(Smell)**
5. The mini-van crashed into the truck with a loud _boom_. **(Sound)**
6. Tyler felt the baseball _whisk_ over his head. **(Sound)**
7. Tammy baked _buttery_ breakfast biscuits. **(Taste)**
8. The Oreo cookie tasted _sweet_ and _crispy_. **(Taste)**
9. Helen sipped on the _creamy_ strawberry milkshake. **(Touch)**
10. Mia pressed the _mushy_ bread dough into the pan. **(Touch)**

Page 23 (Any appropriate sound word will work. See the Sound Word List on page 22)

1. Aliyah tiptoed across the wooden floor. _Creak, Creak._
2. Lorenzo hopped off the slide and landed with a _Thump!_
3. Tam heard the _POP, POP, POP_ of popcorn.
4. _Crash!_ The motorcycle collided with the mini-van.
5. The _whir_ of the airplane engine could be heard above us.
6. The red sports car _screeched_ as it rounded the corner.
7. Grandma's old lawn mower started with a _vroom._
8. The _pitter-patter_ of rain drops woke Giselle up.
9. Marcy could hear the _jingle_ of coins in her change purse.
10. The _rumbling_ of thunder could be heard for miles.

Page 25 (Any appropriate animal sound will work. See the Animal Sound Word List on page 24)

1. The poodle puppy barked, _"Arf, arf, arf!"_
2. The angry lion snarled, _"ROAR!"_
3. The squirrel scurried up the tree squealing, _"Eek, eek, eek!"_
4. Wilbur, the hungry pig, snorted, _"Oink, oink, oink."_
5. The baby bluebird chirped, _"Tweet, tweet."_
6. The gray horse snorted a loud, _"Neigh."_
7. The bumpy bullfrog croaked, _"Ribbit, ribbit."_
8. The rooster greeted the day with a loud, _"Cock-a-doodle-doo!"_
9. The rattlesnake gave a long and low warning, _"Hisssss."_
10. The Siamese kitten mewed, _"Me-ow, me-ow."_

Page 26

1. Go get help! Go! Go! Go! _Go!_
2. Never! Never! _Never_ in a hundred years!
3. We discovered gold! Gold! Precious _gold!_
4. We're rich! We're rich! Rich! Rich! _Rich!_
5. I said no! No, no, _no!_
6. Well done! Well done! _Well done!_
7. The lights flickered on. Off. On. _Off._ On. _Off._

Answer Key

Page 31 (Any appropriate exact verb will work. See the Exact Action Verb List on pages 28-30)

1. Abraham _baked_ a chocolate chip cake. **(Made)**
2. Jane _drove_ to the supermarket to buy groceries. **(Went)**
3. Jason _won_ a gold medal for winning the race. **(Got)**
4. The toddler grabbed the plastic rattle and _hurled_ it. **(Threw)**
5. Mrs. Martell _glanced_ at the student and smiled. **(Looked)**
6. The thief _snatched_ the woman's purse and sprinted away. **(Took)**
7. The eagle _soared_ above the snowy mountains. **(Flew)**
8. Mariel quickly _gobbled_ the pumpkin pie. **(Ate)**
9. Julio _sipped_ the hot chocolate. **(Drank)**
10. Adam _completed_ his homework assignment. **(Did)**

Page 33 (Any appropriate _said_ word will work. See the Said Word List on page 32)

1. "Have a nice day," Manny _yelled_.
2. Elise _asked_, "Does anyone want to play basketball?"
3. The teacher _announced_, "Everyone passed the math test!"
4. "Please don't be late," Danita _grumbled_.
5. "Jamie, let's go!" Melanie _exclaimed_.
6. "I'll buy you lunch today," Edwin _promised_.
7. "Most volunteers work in the morning," Jamal _explained_.
8. "Leave me alone!" _snapped_ Martina.
9. "Be quite. Karsyn is sleeping," _whispered_ Erin.
10. "I'm hungry!" _complained_ Leo.

Page 35 (Any appropriate adverb will work. See the Adverb Word List on page 34)

1. _Yesterday_, the mountain climbers ascended Mt. Everest. **(When)**
2. Avery finished vacuuming _upstairs_. **(Where)**
3. Mona _curiously_ watched the clown enter the room. **(How)**
4. Karina _slowly_ sipped the delicious fruit juice. **(How)**
5. _Carefully_, Ramona climbed into the tree house. **(How)**
6. The tiny yellow duck _effortlessly_ paddled across the lake. **(How)**
7. The softball team _always_ plays on Sundays. **(How often)**
8. Greg _completely_ finished his homework. **(To what extent)**
9. _Tomorrow_, we start our first day of school. **(When)**
10. Marissa _seldom_ finishes her homework on time. **(How often)**

Page 36 (Any appropriate adverb will work. See the Adverb Word List on page 34)

1. _Daringly_, the rescuers climbed the steep cliff.
2. _Yesterday_, Enrique finished the gardening.
3. _Cautiously_, Kayla helped the elderly man cross the street.
4. _Quietly_, Jonah read the last few chapters of _Black Beauty_.
5. _Slowly_, David limped off the soccer field.
6. _Gently_, Kim lifted the crying baby from the crib.
7. _Bravely_, Jayden dove off of the sinking boat into the freezing lake.

52

Answer Key

Page 37 (Any appropriate location word will work See the Location Word List on page 37)

1. Brandon held the tennis racket _over_ his head.
2. Brutus buried his dog bone _under_ the oak tree.
3. The jet soared high _above_ our heads.
4. Dion trotted _around_ the track field.
5. Mom raced _outside_ when she heard the tires screech.
6. A gray poodle puppy darted _across_ the street.
7. Marta tossed her tennis shoes _under_ the table.

Page 39 (Any appropriate interjection will work. See the Interjection Word List on page 38)

1. _Hey_! Let's go swimming today.
2. _Well,_ we can all go to the movies.
3. What did you say, _huh_?
4. _Bummer!_ I can't play because I have to finish my homework.
5. _Really_? Why do you think that?
6. _No,_ I don't want to go shopping right now.
7. _Wow_! That was the best banana milkshake.
8. _Awesome,_ you won the spelling bee!
9. I just can't believe what happen. _Yikes_!
10. _Good morning._ What do you want to do today?

Page 41 (Any appropriate synonym will work. See the Synonym Word List on page 40)

1. Sarah _strolled_ across the dance floor. **(Walked)**
2. Lori _sprinted_ around the track two times. **(Ran)**
3. Mina _adored_ her new poodle puppy. **(Liked)**
4. Gerard _whacked_ the punching bag as hard as he could. **(Hit)**
5. The doctor _examined_ the injury on the teenager's leg. **(Looked)**
6. Jose was _excited_ about his report card. **(Happy)**
7. The _worn_ jacket was falling apart. **(Old)**
8. The _enormous_ elephant lived in the jungle. **(Big)**
9. Melinda _gobbled_ the chocolate chip cookies. **(Ate)**
10. Katie _discovered_ a buried treasure in the sand. **(Found)**

Page 41-Bottom (Any appropriate synonym will work)

Jana **visited** the zoo on Friday. First, she **walked** over to see the jungle animals. There was a **huge** elephant name Jumbo and a **tall** giraffe named Ella. She **watched** while Jumbo **grazed on** grass and Ella **nibbled on** tree leaves. When the animals **spotted** Jana, both **wandered** over to the fence and **stared** at her. Jana wondered if they **craved** the chocolate candy bar she was **chewing**. Before Jana could **place** the candy bar in her purse, Jumbo **snatched** it with his trunk and **offered** it to Ella.

Answer Key

Page 43 (Any appropriate antonym will work. See the Antonym Word List on page 42)

1. Sumi's room was **clean**, but Jocelynn's room was _messy_.
2. Juan loves **piping-hot** chocolate, but Maria prefers _ice-cold_ tea.
3. Polar bears like **cool** temperatures while camels live in _warm_ climates.
4. Janet quickly **sped** around the _slow_ moving truck.
5. The elephant was **huge**, but the mouse was _tiny_.
6. The lime was **bitter**, but the strawberries were _sweet_.
7. Kyra's parents were **rich**, but Megan's family was _poor_.
8. Jayden liked to stay **active** while Max was often _lazy_.
9. Maria spoke in a **whisper**, but Dina _screamed_.
10. Nina **gobbled** the fruit cake while Maya _nibbled_ on the grapes.

Page 45 (Any appropriate time order word will work. See the Time Order Word List on page 44)

1. Finally, Corey worked his way to the front of the lunch line.
2. Before long, Jamison reached the top of the huge hill.
3. After a long wait, Ming decided to walk home.
4. First, we have to press the cookie dough onto the baking sheet.
5. Meanwhile, Justin will play guitar while he waits.
6. At times, Wanda wondered if she should give up.
7. Shortly after sunrise, the rooster crowed.
8. Soon, it was time to leave for school.
9. At midnight, the grandfather clock chimed.
10. When the school year ended, the students celebrated their graduation.

Recommended Resources

Bingham, Darlene Dehart. *Punctuate Like a Pro!* San Bernardino, 2017.

On Line Dictionary. 2017. http://www.dictionary.com.

On Line Thesaurus. 2017. http://www.thesaurus.com.

www.ingramcontent.com/pod-product-compliance
Lightning Source LLC
Chambersburg PA
CBHW080532030426
42337CB00023B/4704